My Private Room
I opened the door, and there was light…

Cheryl Katherine Wash

EbonyEnergy Publishing, Inc. (NFP)
A division of the GEM Literary Foundation
Chicago, Illinois

Copyright©2002
Cheryl Katherine Wash

All rights reserved. Printed and bound in the United States of America. No part of this book may be reproduced or utilized in any form or by any means, electronic or mechanical, including photocopying, recording, or by any information storage or retrieval system except by a reviewer who may quote brief pages in a review to be printed in a magazine or newspaper, without permission in writing from the publisher. Inquiries to be addressed to the following:

EbonyEnergy Publishing, Inc. (NFP)
A Division of the GEM Literary Foundation
Permissions Department
P.O. Box 43476
Chicago, IL 60643-0476

Although the author and publisher have made every effort to ensure the accuracy and completeness of information contained in this book, we assume no responsibility for errors, inaccuracies, omissions or any inconsistency therein.

Any slights of people, places belief systems or organizations are unintentional. Any resemblance to any living, dead or somewhere in between is truly coincidental unless otherwise noted.

ISBN: 0-9722795-0-4
Library of Congress Control Number: 2002094082

Cover Design: Erik Stenberg
Technical Support: Rasaki Solebo

Printed in the United States
Third Printing

EbonyEnergy Publishing
www.EbonyEnergyPublishing.com
P.0. Box 43476
Chicago, IL 60643-0476

Acknowledgments

First of all I would like to acknowledge and thank God! I am blessed to have been introduced to the spirit long before I knew that the spirit is not only above, below and around us but resides in each and everyone of us. We are *all* expressions of God and created in His image and likeness.

Then there is you. There are so many who helped me to reach this point and, I wish I could include a personal thanks to each and every one of you. Believe me, I realize that you are out there, and I will always remember that God sends people into our lives for reasons that may or may not be obvious to us now or may remain transparent to us forever. But, again, I want to thank you for the experiences that have influenced me mentally, physically and spiritually while I continue on my journey toward inner peace.

Blessed are those who are pure in heart
for they shall see God.

(St. Matthew 5:8)

To My Creator

Almighty God

and

My Loving Parents

James and Sheley Katherine

Table of Contents

An Angel's Poem (11)
The Wonderful (12)
The Old Neighborhood (13)
The Color of Wind (14)
Cool Water Grave (15)
Are You Stuck in a Rut? (16)
Occupational Cramps (17)
It's Only One Tear, Dear (18)
The Rocker (19-20)
The Fruit Poem (21)
Rainbows and Dreams (22)
Emptiness (23)
Footing Your Dream (24)
The Red Rose (25)
Love Magic (26)
I Have a Dream Too (27)
The Lover (28)
Togetherness (29)
Lover's Lane (30)
I Lost Love (31-32)
No More (33)
Hot Enough For Iced Tea (34)
Two Faces of Love (35)
My Grass (36)
The Chase (37)
Programmed Humans (38)
We will be as One (39)
What Is Love? (40)
Tardy (41)
Chicago Vocational High School (42)
Confusion (43)
A Common Whore (44)
I Got the Blues (45)
The Bus Driver (46-47)
The Windy City (48)

Table of Contents Continued...

The Day After (49)
Let Him Be Himself (50-51)
No Us (52)
A Lazy Sun (53)
Beyond Repair (54)
Jesus (55)
Let's Dance (56)
You (57)
Them Eggs...Them Eggs... (58)
Thinking of You (59)
Magic Touch (60)
I AM? (61)
My Gift (62)
Escape to Nowhere (63)
Unknown (64)
You Nurture Me (65)
Send My Love (66)
No More Monsters (67)
Spring (68)
Second Time Around (69)
Our Calendar (70)
The Scary Hair Story (71-73)
Green-Eyed Monster (74)
IT (75)
The Good Life (76)
Doomed to Die (77)
Stop Lying (78)
Adolescence (79)
Punishment (80)
Crazy Thoughts (81)
Go For It (82)
Chocolate Covered Nut (83)
Why Life? (84)
I'd Freed the Truth (85)
It's Not Over (86)

Table of Contents Continued...

Escribo/Escribi (87)
Lost in Oz (88)
Euphoria-Rastafarian Love (89)
I Can't Stand The Rain (90)
Our Portrait (91)
Precious Gems (92)
The World from My Room (93)

Introduction

My Private Room is a collection of poetry, expressions, and images viewed through the windows of my soul. I entitled this collection *My Private Room* because I believed that I had to control how different experiences made me feel when I was around other people. I felt that being able to control my feelings made me a stronger individual.

I would free all of my repressed emotions by way of pen and paper once my parents tucked me away in bed in my little room-my private room.

I was metaphysically stimulated by the world and gifted to see beyond what first appears. My feelings were tuned to and deeply moved by negative and positive experiences. I would re-create them on paper as soon as I settled into my room.

I was a very private person growing up when it came to expressing how I really saw the world and the purpose of people and spirits that dwell in the universe, I used to hide my poetry. I felt that if someone read my work he/she would be able to read me, or the person may feel that it was inspired by him/her.

I remember wanting to appear happy at all times, especially when a relationship was not going well or a love I had lost. Well, that was before I matured and opened the door to my private room and saw the light.

Although the brightness appeared blinding, an amazing positive energy kept pushing me forward. Walking out of darkness into light was an incredibly exhilarating experience. It was easier to remain in the comfort of my private room, which today I call fear.

Once I saw the light outside of my door, I knew that I had nothing to fear but fear itself. I began to share my thoughts and feelings with others and realized that the same views and personal experiences on new and lost loves, children, society, politics, death, nature, pursuing dreams, and life in general are felt by many.

Many parents today continue to deny their children the right to express their thoughts and emotions freely without fear of retribution and humiliation, which can stifle creativity and lead to repressed emotions. We need to encourage our children to freely express themselves, which will help eliminate anger, hatred and depression and spread love and positive energy throughout the universe.

Well, once I saw the light and began my soul searching and spiritual healing during my journey toward inner peace, I went back and gathered poetry that I had written years ago as well as some of my more recent works and decided to publish a volume of poems and other musings to share with other kindred spirits.

Please open your eyes, ears, mind, heart, and soul as you enter. I am sure that each of you will find positive and inspirational messages and themes that are enveloped in each message throughout the collection as you take an intimate look inside *My Private Room*.

An Angel's Poem

On a good day….
A little Angel in heaven was in a poetic mood
The desire to create something unique started to brew
There had to be a way to personify nature and poetry
With the help of the Almighty Lord, they created thee
The Lord blew breath into this perfect human shell
Leaving the details for the little angel to perform well

Your forehead is the flight of the eagle soaring high
Your eyes are the dreamy and dark night sky
Your voice is the melodious song of the meadowlark
Your twinkling dimples are the stars on the darkest night
Your lovely smile is the morning sun shining bright
Your cheekbones are symbolic for structure and control

Tall like giant redwood trees, including strong and bold
Fast and powerful as the Great Plains buffalo on the run
Mannerism of clouds rolling softly across the horizon
Mirror Shakespearean sonnets and Egyptians pyramids
Created by a little angel in heaven by the name of Cupid

Will forever spread your love to all and be loved by me
You are emotions to be recollected in tranquility
My little Angel sent to spread love and inner peace
You, my dear, are what God, the angels and I call poetry

The Wonderful

In the beginning
Before I met you
There were storms-Quiet storms
Then I met you…
My life became instantly calm
Something was wonderful
Sunshine and laughter
A rainbow beginning and...
Full of colors
Pastel shades-like parades
A new dream-started to grow
Each dream harder to climb
I wanted to succeed-I strove harder
To reach the end-an end
An unknown end
Maybe cold-maybe the untold
Or something else...
Maybe wonderful
You touched me one day
Out of my dreams-In my dreams
You touched my heart
My Valentine's sweetheart
Every day is a new start
I reached the top of the bright
Only masses of color-no borders
Sliding slowly downward
Then faster to the end
Of the wonderful
Then I landed softly
On something warm
Something bright
Something colorful
Something wonderful
The wonderful you...

The Old Neighborhood

the curbs are full
of paper and trash
the air smells like disease
kitchens with dingy walls
smeared and
stained with grease
the gangster leans never
give them whiplash
the old playground
no longer looks good
no swings on the set
a cat screeches and
scratches at dinner
–a fat rat
mutt dogs run in packs
no chains
no tags
no owner
gangs controlling
every street corner
hoops with no nets
gang writing on the walls
smelly urine in halls
courts with no balls
boxes with no sand
a switchblade
just sliced
the old beggar's hand
broken glass on sidewalks
boarded-up windows
and doors
midnight summons the
young whores
fat swollen overused lips
stink-
and painted in cheap
shades of pink
crack and smack keeps
them all whacked
only can relate to hitting
the sack
in time they lack
in money they slack
front yards
don't grow grass
backyards breed weeds
and hash wet babies
crying from their diaper
rashes the drugs have
burned and turned
their mommies into scary
zombies empty bottles
smell of liquor
the hot links and
deep-fried polish
sausages make
their 'stank' figures
thicker
some still jamming
in the back
of a yesterday's Cadillac
with them mean gangster
leans and those super
clean white walls
we let our gold mold
we were tall
how did we fall
we once had it all

The Color of Wind

Feel the relaxing breeze of the wind on your skin on the hottest summer day

See how it sails the child's kite high in your eyes across the deep vanilla-blue sky

Smell the scents of flowers and trees in its cool sweet breeze as it whirls by

Hear the howling of this uncontrollable dynamic force that comes from astray

Taste the power of the wind that can please and destroy within the same hour

Cool Water Grave

Her thoughts run deep
And end at ocean blue
It's waiting calmly for her
A place to end her sins
'Tombstoneless' cemetery
Mirrors her distorted face
Her face still lacks grace
In a wave of cool graves
A reflection
of gin and sin
Lover and user
of many men
Ambiguous
liar denier crier
Lost alone
in a cruel maze
Exhausted
weary and dazed
She thinks the cool water
Will cleanse
her cursed soul
End the nightmares
and dreams
Water feels so
cold and chilly
Now she freezes
and begins to see
Life was not as bad
as it seemed
No one heard her cry then or now
As her mouth and soul releases...
Bubbles of drowned screams...
Bubbles full of silent blue screams...

Are You Stuck in a Rut?

Are you so confused?
That you want to cry
Sometimes die…
You feel like you need to fly
You need to run
Stay tangled in some drunken fun
Hiss at the loyalty of the holy nuns
Kiss all of your commitments
Your duties
Your responsibility
Your obligations
Good-bye and farewell
Go to hell!
And you really mean it
This time...
No reneging
On this feeling
You are really digging it
Think you are about to groove
But you are afraid to move
Hell, no! Won't go!
Another moon has passed
Another sun has risen
Your place of dwelling
Has become your prison
Still there with a blank stare
Still full of fear
Full of confusion
Suffering from illusions
To get to a conclusion
And to get out of the rut
Stop making excuses and
Saying but...
Just do it...Just do it...Just do it...

Occupational Cramps

I want to be a skipper
But, I am startled by the sea
I want to be a gardener
But, I am terrified of bees
I want to be a stunt driver
But, I am horrified of cars
I want to be an astronaut
But, I am frightened of Mars
I want to be a mountain climber
But, I am scared of heights
I want to be a kamikaze
But, I am afraid to fight
I guess I can become a writer
Because…I am not apprehensive to write

It's Only One Tear, Dear

Today he cried one tear
for the first time he can
see, hear, smell and taste the rain
and to him it feels quite strange, more like pain
as he moves closer to see clearer–
his lonely face in the cracked mirror
an image like the painting of the sad clown
that you see at the circus or around town…with one tear
while she is now feeling like a queen,
smiling and holding a glass of spirits that's crystal clear
she cheers, with her new true love
who winks at her as he sips at the foam of a
cool beer after they toast-then to the terrace
to have a cool and relaxing smoke
while back at the home that he broke
the lump gathers in his throat, 'cause he knew
she was indeed true…Now he feels like
he needs to cry or he will choke
now his heart is broken, heart is
full of pain, full of emotion over a
love lost 'cause now she has the potion
now in real life–He only cried one tear
but it doesn't fall…
Is there an invisible barrier? A wall?
It just oozed out of one eye and began to stall
and that tear is beginning to swell
oh well, one tear for all her years of crying
from all of his lying and of an old love dying
now she is all sunny and bright inside
she has no more weeping eyes
she has no more watery eyes
she has no more wet pillows
she no more feeling like a weeping willow...
while he cries his only...one lonely tear...

The Rocker

There she goes
pacing again
Rocking again...
Over thinking-sinking
Tears of fear
fill up the eyes
No blinking, the tears
won't fall
No peeking. Let her be...
As she stares at
the bleak walls
Afraid to walk.
Rather talk.
Talk mess. Talk jive.
Talk dreams

Hang up the phone and
let out a few screams...
She's a rocker, not a
mover, not a shaker…
Look at the valuable
wedding ring...
No longer
means a thing....
The higher power,
in them-
She has to keep believing
In order to keep weaving
Through this
sticky web of
What some call life. Her
word-*Strife*

Then she starts to think
Her plan, her
accomplishments
The love of her life
They all stink
As her no-longer lover
passes without a blink
Like yellowed newspaper
Old news, history, like
yesterday

Stuck in a rut
All y'all. Y'all hear me?
Y'all too...Bunch of lanes
Catching gutter balls
Like Y'all lives
don't suck!
She screams these attacks
Silently in her dreams.
Again, the darn
thinking.....
Oh no, now she's seeing
Too little results
She goes from sane to
insane
To sane to the brain
All over again
A circle
Gonna take a miracle
She's traveled around the
world 360 degrees.

She's back And never
seen a coconut tree
No trees in her world

Afraid of that other world
The real deal
Thinking about getting
killed
So she stays put...
Safe...
Say a grace...
While still thinking...

To make nothing to
something
That will be nothing
again
She goes from free to
bound
To freedom again
She is tired…no wheels
She is not moving.
Just sitting here thinking
And rocking
She is not a mover

She is not a shaker
Her motion is back and
forth
Not a forward thrust...
Not like a rocket. No
bang!
Hush. She's thinking.
She's just rocking
Thinking and rocking
Rocking and thinking
Thinking and rocking
Rocking and
thinking about...
Who she should be...
What she should be...
When she should be...
Where she should be...
How she should be...
While she is rocking...and
thinking...
She rocks...She thinks…
She thinks…She rocks...
She thinks…thinks…and
rocks…and rocks…

The Fruit Poem

Let us pray for the sun and rain and
the farmers who planted all of the peach,
mango, plum, apple and orange trees

Go wash some fruit from the bowl
on the table in the dining room
so we can begin our ritual to consume

Cover me in strawberries,
cherries, berries and bananas-
colors of the toucan and the brilliant canary

Color me with your desired flavor
for your savor-whether it is all the
exact same fruit or mismatch

Leave a little fruit in the bowl
to eat during our secret
nights when the erotic exotic
and fruit blend taste just right

Rainbows and Dreams

dreams are like rainbows
some believe in them
some don't
some will
some won't
some follow their dreams
until they find a pot
at the end of the rainbow
others give up
but you should never give up
dreams have nothing
to do with luck
dreams are like
the sun, amazing...
shining...warming...
after a rainy cloudy day
dreams are like heartaches
when they don't come true
as long as you believe–
another vision and love
will get you through
you never want to lose vision
of your dreams
so remember, dreams are like rainbows
they only appear after the rain

Emptiness

they still feel alone
although married with kids
living under one roof
feels like a wound
their broken home
like an empty cocoon

with a super Band-aid
lots of first-aid
still growing apart
holding on to little bits and
pieces of each other's
disappointed hearts

things are not as they thought
not as they believed it should be
making it hard to leave
hard to say goodbye
hard to cry and
hard to not cry

things are not as they wished
not as they dreamed
not as they said
not as they promised
on their wedding day
as they approached
their sacred honeymoon bed

not as they now pretend
they want to believe their love is still tight
and all is going to be all right
even though this is not the beginning
it is the beginning of the end
but to the truth they have to face, but when?

Footing Your Dream

Don't worry about change
things may or may not stay the same
Stay focused on your dream and
put one foot in front of the other...

Don't let your dream be greater
than your dedication to the dream...
You need to set little goals that
would be little pieces of your dream
and if they change, the ultimate end will not.

If you keep calling your dream
a dream and do not set goals
or milestones and take the necessary steps,
your dream will always be a dream
that you experience when you are sound asleep...

The Red Rose

The red of a rose is like fire…
a heart's desire

a single rose
is just as intense
as the rosebush
against a white
picket fence

the prickly thorns
always on their job
trying to no avail
to prevent from
being mobbed and robbed

the beautiful petals
shimmering after
an April shower

the most divine
of all flowers
because of the rain's power
roses give pleasures
to eyes and noses

there is nothing more
satisfying than giving
or receiving a bouquet
of roses they are a blessing to
have on earth, invaluable are their worth

Love Magic

the fullness of love
the nothingness of love
the mysteries of love
the temporary moments of love

how can anyone feel alone or cannot
find love in a world so vast and so busy
so many millions trillions zillions
gazillions of people

love is so rare and hard to come by
and many can't find love in one person
that will equate them to a god or goddess
or someone higher

love is like smoke, it takes every breath,
it takes life, and then vanishes into thin air,
love is like a cloud you see it
gray but it is blue

you can see love but you can't grab it
you go right through it like driving
through fog like an airplane in the sky plowing
through visuals called nothingness

I Have a Dream Too

Martin Luther King had a dream…
To you what does that dream mean?
To me it's a dream that everyone should be free
If you were living then you could plainly see
That these times are not as they used to be then
You can easily have all shades of the rainbow as friends
All cultures and races are moving higher in society
Jobs and opportunities are now at a variety
We are not quite where we want to be
But, no more genocide - like Holocaust and slavery
We should all have a vision like Martin Luther King
Because each and everyone of us has a dream

The Lover

With a great lover you experience
more than you meant to share

While the love is enlightenment to
some and others are being driven insane

A great lover will make you answer
when your lover asks you questions
during passionate moments like....
What's my name? What's my name?

A super lover can make you scream
out his name while you are with
another lover

A lost lover will send you around the world
to find another lover or to escape the feeling
of the lost lover

When a lover is gone or has done wrong,
you will let the world through your arms
in search of another lover who can love
you the same

A lover can be the grounds of you missing new
lovers because you remain bitter or have you
selling your soul for the heated feeling of your
best lover again

Togetherness

You, my love, have a deep love for words as on the contrary you tell me that love is felt and not heard

Since you have this love for words and you need to express your feelings you told me that you will try to explain at your best

Love having no color, shape, form or fashion but so thrilling, fulfilling are these abstract moments of passion

Originating in the heavens and sent down through our souls, Love will ultimately make warm what is harsh and bitter cold

You told me that love is more precious than many pots of gold and to consider it a gift because to some it is impossible to hold

Love cannot be compared to gifts or bought with money. You must cherish

and protect love naturally as the bees do honey

You'll feel my love whether I am near or far because I feel your energy mentally, physically and spiritually, my sweet darling dear

When we must part for a day, there is no reason to have fear because tomorrow will come and our love will reunite and cheer

We feel that we are in love and we are not wrong in our feelings and thoughts. True love is what we are when togetherness is all that we sought

Lover's Lane

You are driving down a highway all the same
Then your sweetheart turns off onto a narrow lane
This deep wooded area isn't officially on the route
It's a place where your first love takes you to make out
You're feeling special and give this haven a nice name
Then you find out that he has taken all your friends to what
Is known as Lover's Lane…

I Lost Love

I am lost…

a feeling that
you are unable
to formulate words

to describe
a feeling that once
had a drive, a plan, a destination

a feeling that once
had determination
anticipation
imagination
recreation
direction
erection

a feeling that is
no longer a feeling
a feeling that is lost

I am lost without the feeling
I am lost without the love
lost love

I am lost
you lost
we lost

the first time
love is lost
is like the first time

your father
left your mother…

the first time a child is
abandoned
by its mother…
unforgettable
regrettable
a lost that will
change your
outlook on life
on love
on trust
forever
and ever
and ever
and ever

No More

No more frost-bitten toes,
No more runny noses,
No more slippery streets,
No more boots on feet,
No more coughing and sneezing,
No more standing and freezing,
No more snow the winter can bring
No more; because, it's time for spring

Hot Enough for Iced Tea

It's June and I am very hot
anxiously I wait for a breeze
that has come not

as I sit in my gazebo and think about
what I now know and where I want
to go while …making an attempt to
enhance my writing skills

this hot weather is going
against my power and will
it is too hot to do anything,
especially think

it is too hot for me to give
my gorgeous neighbor Johnny Boy
a wink when he has just noticed
my summer wear, which is hot pink

my dog and cat are under the porch fast asleep
I start to dream of some cold iced tea
and seas that are cool bluish green and deep

at last a cool breeze blows though the openings
in my swing and in my B*etter Homes and Garden* gazebo
cools me off, the cat and dog, for a hot
moment then away the blowing wind goes

now the clock has a quarter after three
the cool evening is not approaching
fast enough for me

'cause in about fifteen more minutes
then I am on my way into the house
for some cold and extra-sweet iced tea

Two Faces of Love

Love can be tricky
like pain

simultaneously
nurturing
by giving some life

while across town
taking away
someone else's life
as a result
of lost love…

love washes away
pain

while love brings pain
love is more
complex than

an oxymoron…
sun
moon
day
night

my only-only love
can become
my only-only hate
or already is my only love
or only hate…

My Grass

In the summer my grass grows such a
pretty winter green, from miles around
it can be easily seen

My grass is thick like a forest wall and my grass
grows so tall because I won't cut it at all

And from my porch I don't get scorched
it blocks the sunrays on the sunniest of days

I miss my grass on the bitter-cold winter days
and wish my grass and summer would never go away

The Chase

Love is a feeling that you sense, is far more
granular than one can formulate in words

love is the biggest
the cleverest expression of emotions

love can intoxicate your mind into this false hope that this
will be the one

love has the most disguises
love is deeper than just a feeling

hot, cold
sweet, sour
bath or shower

no matter how we nurture love
for it comes then goes
and this we all know

love hurts more than hate
love is that is more powerful than a drug
a bad habit, can't quit, can't break
can't stop the chase

I keep looking for this feeling
or a temporary fix
the high
the come down
the remorse
the recovery
the tears
the temporary discovering
and then you are back chasing it again

Programmed Humans

I walk, I talk, I smile
Oh, what a machine I am
I listen, I do
I never express what I am feeling
Whether it is good, bad or blue
I do this and that
I obey and never have open chats
I will breed little ones
Do I program them too?
Oh, well, that is how
We humans who are programmed do!

We will be as one

There is a reason
For thoughts at hand
For I lost a very special man
He meant a whole lot to me
Please listen to my story
When I met him, I knew I was in love
All the beautiful things I every dreamed of
I wanted us to have the best relationship in the world
For him never to be taken by any girl
He was all of my dreams come true
If I lost him, I knew I would be blue
We had many great times together
I thought our love would last forever
We started getting into silly fights
Never did we think the other was right
We could not stay angry at each other long
At times we felt when we were wrong
Soon we were both trying to be in command
For I was turning a woman and him a man
We were so much in love that we grew fond
And something soon had to break the bond
The day before the terrible split
His kiss I thought I would always get
I can't explain what broke up our relationship
But, it is over and not even a friendship
I'll love him always and forever
And I promise, separated or together
I wonder does he suffer too
He should feel as I do
I've been miserable ever since we've been apart
I hope I'll soon recover from the broken heart
Without him life isn't fun
By the end of time…we'll be as one

What Is Love?

pose this question to your family, friends
mentors…

what is love?

ask the greatest philosophers, teachers, preachers
what is love…ask the richest, the poorest, the fast,
the slow, the smartest to the not so smartest

everyone thinks they know what love is but can they
give me an answer the question that I can't
seem to answer for myself

they will probably respond that the
question is rhetorical But I still feel that …

no formula
no wizard
no geniuses
no one

can give a clear-cut answer or help me find
the perfect solution to this thing called love

but they all swear
they have the answer
but they all swear
they're living the answer
but they all swear
they have been in love
but they all swear
they are still in love…
but, I swear they don't know what love is…

Tardy

Baby girl, you must rush, rush, rush
Or you will miss the yellow school bus
It's Monday morning–look at the date
Oh Mighty Lord, help us not to be late
It is time for school oh, what a fool I am
You have an exam instead we ate Honey Baked ham
And I let you play video games all night on the TV
Instead of studying for your finals and spelling bee
We missed the bus - now we must run and that's no fun
Baby girl, it is tough being you! What're we going to do?
Over there is your school… Don't be tardy is a rule!
Getting up late will make you and me both sorry
Buzz, there goes the bell-Baby girl, you are tardy!

Chicago Vocational High School

I remember C.V.S. was a great school to attend
The teachers and students were the best of friends
The attractive school colors were blue and gold
They meant a lot because we were strong and bold
Many students had pride and were always true
They did not want their futures to be blue
Not many came to school to laugh and fool around
There were only a few whose grades were a big let down
Not anyone could be accepted at the big C.V.S.
Freshmen, sophomores, juniors, and seniors did their best
A true family in student activities, sports and games
Chicago Vocational is in my personal 'Hall of Fame'

Confusion

What is this stuff you keep talking about?
What is this pain all about?
You feel like you are suffering
Plenty of confusion and illusions
This disease many call dreaming
The result most call failing
Derailing like a train in a wreck
Thrown off course…off track
Your dreams are taking longer to achieve
A feeling of not going anywhere
But you continue to believe
There is more to life than just being
A static being without a dream
But you are still stuck in the middle
Of nowhere at this time…suspended
There are voices telling you that life
Could be worse...
Could be unknown...
Could be better…
Why can't you just be satisfied?
Instead you cry
Instead you cry
Instead you cry
Now with that done…wipe your weepy eyes
Continue to try
Continue to try
Continue to try
And keep the faith
You will lose your confusion...and win…

A Common Whore

Sugar, if you have the money, call on me
I'm great. Give me your loot. Satisfaction guaranteed
I will give you great times for your pay
You have to believe what I am here to say
I got the power to turn your world upside-down
Just ask the men who call me to clown around
They use me as a plaything or handy tool
I am not a court jester or your average fool
I am not on drugs; but, my family needs money
Little education and low paying jobs 'ain't' funny
I have no idea what the word 'luv' really means
A respected queen and loved by a true king
Sometimes - I am attacked, beaten and abused
My job is a risk, I know my body can be bruised
Men don't care if I am infected with viruses or disease
Doesn't matter if, in their breeze, I cough, fart or sneeze
Keep rubbing filthy hands and dirty money all over me
I pray for change or death will be set me free
For you and friends to come, I have no house, floor or door
My home is the street corner, I am the common whore
I know my money making job is a downright sin
This is how my life started...Is this how it will end?

I Got the Blues

I feel dark inside like the color blue
I spent my life loving you
You spent yours being untrue
Yeah...you are not true
Yes. You are not true
And...yes! I am so blue
Some call it the blues
And yeah, I call it the blues too...

The Bus Driver

I only thought it would be a typical day
A day away from the office to relax
An outing…A trip
We boarded this big bus
Nothing real serious
But I felt like something
Was mysterious
The skies were powder blue
Then it happened
The driver's face
I saw the driver's face mirrored
In the rearview
His face was a magnet
Don't know what kind of a magnet…
A chic magnet
A lust magnet
A love magnet-
It instantly attracted myself
My innermost vulnerable self
My mind started to wonder
Wondering about his life
His wife
Himself
Myself
He travels the highways
Interstate, intrastate and tri-state
The Midwest states
He meets more people in a day
Than some do in weeks
He meets more women
Than a Laundromat
Some nice, some cheat, some big, some fat
To me he's a king
King of the road
King of the traveling way

To me he's like a precious stone
Or like the Emperor of Rome
You can only see him passing
Can never touch him
Can never own him
You can cherish him
Praise him from afar
You can cherish the moment
That your eyes laid upon him
And take a mental picture of
His smile, his cool style,
His handsome profile
And place it forever in your heart
He is my Midwest man
He is my Midwest guy
Just when I think I've gotten over him
A charter bus passes by
I instantly smile at first
Then my smile slowly melts away
Because I am hurt
Because his face continues to haunt
My heart
How long will I wish for him?
How long will I cry for him?
Will I slowly die inside for him?
Only time will tell
Whether or not I will escape this hell
I cannot tell
I just can't tell
But I will wonder
I will always wonder
Will we ever meet….
On the road again?.

The Windy City

A fast city where the wind is known to blow
Chicago is the Windy City as the saying goes
There are many beautiful attractions to see
Lake Shore Drive, the parks, birds and trees
Like everywhere else Chicago has its challenged parts
But they are being renovated because of the good hearts
The communities do a lot to improve the inner city
This is why Chicago is a high-ranking city
Chicago may not be the largest city in the U.S.
First, second, third, we will always be the best
Chicago also has Michigan–a great lake
To enjoy its water walking along the shore is all it takes
Downtown Chicago has many stores from which to shop
Stage shows and movies are in such a variety
Magnificent Mile and Gold Coast is high society
Navy Pier, Sears Tower and Buckingham Fountain
Big enough for me, so who needs a mountain?
Chicago will always be the best around
Chicago will always be my kind of town

The Day After

they were all alone before the education
all alone before the career
all alone before the stunning wardrobe
all alone before the shining gems
all alone before the hilltop mansion
all alone before the fancy car
all alone before the fairytale wedding
all alone before the family dog
all alone before the picture-perfect family
all alone before the fancy invitations
all alone before the get-away vacations
all alone before the galas and social events
they are still alone after all that has been mentioned
so their loneliness before and after hurts all the same

Let Him Be Himself

He is alone in this crowded room
Everyone is laughing.
He can hear the questions coming...
Who are you?
What do you do?
Then he can feel the responses.
The defensive responses to prove he is somebody
And then when he tells them who
Someone else told
him to be
They smile, they get close
They want to feel if what he says has been
Materialized...specialized…crystallized
What kind of car you drive?
Where do you live?
Who are your friends? Are they in high places?
Can you get me some comp tickets?
The hook-up? Do you own a Cadillac Truck?
How many bathrooms?
How many rooms?
Any income property?
What was the most exotic vacations?
He is surrounded because he has mastered
The answers…
Even though he is calm and poised on the outside
He is all alone on the inside.
He can fool them. He knows this game.
Alone because the matter at hand
Is that everything he told them is true
However, his possessions and his
Accomplishments are ranked
And the higher the ranking the
Bigger the crowd. The groupies.
The goofs. The leeches.
However, he is surrounded.

He has their attention.
They want to get his contact information.
A business card. A connection.
He is in a crowded room,
But he is still alone.
Even though he is who he is
If he gives up the career, the car,
The house, and the savvy conversation
He will no longer be in the middle of
A crowd in the spotlight
He will be alone. Just as he is now.
All alone...in this overcrowded room

No Us

When I think of us
What happened to us
We used to dream
Now I dream
Alone on our team
Or my team
Now, it's only me
Say what?
No us!
When I think of us
What happened to us
We used to dream
We were two on a team
Now I dream
All alone
What a lonely team
Alone on what used
To be our team
Our dream
Now my team
It's only me
Only me

A Lazy Sun

The sun refused
to shine today
some people are
not as happy and gay
inside the adults must stay
but the children continue to play

Some say that it is
not fair that today
the sun didn't do its job
Our hot summer day has
just been robbed

The sun let the
dreadful rain fall
and some didn't
appreciate it at all

The flowers and trees
had a celebration
for them it was a day
of recreation

The sad people were
very wet and upset
their hairstyles and
clothes got soaking wet

Just look at the big picture
and you will see clearer on
rainy and cloudy days

Because I love the sun whether
it shines or not for it's a very
positive source of energy that we've got

Beyond Repair

No longer is the love winning
They are all about pretending
No longer understanding
or comprehending
No longer befriending
No more bending
The roses he stopped sending
When they come through the door
No more are they grinning
When they are out in the streets
We both are sinning
Was their love lost from the beginning?
Is this really the beginning of an ending?
Let's pray that their love stage is never beyond mending...

Jesus

Once upon a time a man named Jesus came to town
People teased him like he was a circus clown
There were good folk who loved to see Him around
Because Jesus never did anything bad, not even a frown
The children knew he was very kind
And when they wanted to play he didn't mind
They said He was a mild-mannered and quiet fellow
And over His head was a glowing halo
One sunny day evil people forced Jesus to leave
The people of the town thought it was hard to believe
When the little children found out they all cried
It was shocking to them but no one died
So Jesus left the physical world but we see Him in
our spiritual world every day

Let's Dance

Take my hand
and dance with me
set my heart, my mind, my
body free, let my soul
know that you are a kindred
spirit who truly and
kindly wants to dance
with me

Take my hand
and dance with
me because I have
been sitting and
waiting for this
dance for so long
let's dance so you can
cradle me and touch me
the way nature's mother
massages her unborn
child still in the womb
with a vision of the
miracle dancing in her head

Take my hand
and dance with me
let's dance all night long
let's dance so close
that the air that exists
in the space between us
suffocates and can't breathe
and we'll move slow
like tonight is forever and there
is no tomorrow and
the end of the nightingale's
song will never, ever come...

You

I have loved you from the day my eyes, which are the window to my soul, caught a glimpse of the tall, dark and handsome you

We have been through our ups and downs and we have not always been to our love true

But we have been there for each other because we both know we were meant to be together

Life will continue to bring us painstaking trials and tribulations, which will test us but keep us bonded forever

There were times that I wished everything could be just perfect and peachy keen as in a movie scene

But life has shown me that no matter how we dream some things are as real as they seem

The lesson that I learned is that as of this day forward I will cherish our moments as if they could be the last in the time we share together

Because our physical and earth life have us living on borrowed time and while our spiritual life is forever

I will continue to pray that we can forget about all of the negative past and thank God that we still have forever to look forward to

Happy Valentine's Day, honey dearest, I love you!

Them Eggs...Them Eggs...

Why do we put our trust in this one individual?
Like the packer and grocer put all them eggs
In one carton and all them eggs on one shelf
In the store…
Like the country woman who put all her eggs
In the nice straw basket then falls…
The one emotion called love
What happened to the saying of not
Putting all of your eggs in one basket…
Someone dropped the basket
Now my big heart was dropped and broken
Into dozens of little pieces
Just like them eggs…
Just like them eggs...
No one sells
No one buys
Cracked
Broken
Rotten eggs…
They just sit on the shelf
All by themselves
And rot
And rot
And rot
Like my heart sits
In my chest
A pitiful mess
And them eggs–
They begin to smell
My eyes swell
Like rotten eggs
My broken heart
Is just like them eggs
Them broken eggs

Thinking of You

When I think of you
always goes my woe
all of my dreams come true

When I think of you
I am no longer sad
I am no longer mad
at the deep blue skies
as I wipe my watery eyes
for taking you away
and leaving me astray

When I think of you
I feel that you are still here
my love, my only wish is that
I can fly like a dove
so I could visit with
you in the heavens above

When I think of you...

Magic Touch

If you try to play your cards right
Everything might finally be all right
You treat me as if you don't love me
If we part you eventually will see
To many, I am an African Beauty Queen
But to you, I am the girl of your dreams
Open your heart to how much I love you
Our love is special, our love is true
Why are you pushing us apart?
Must you try to break my heart?
If you feel as if you no longer love me
Free our love, I may be a lock, you have the key
Don't fool me and have me waiting for you long
It will only hurt me more and be downright wrong
If we part, I'll love you still as much
I want to stay together forever
Only you have the magic touch

I AM?

WHAT AM I?
AM I
LEARNING WHAT
I AM
OR WHAT AM I?
I AM
I THINK I AM
WHAT YOU TOLD ME TO BE
I AM
I AM A BLACK WOMAN
I AM BLACK
I AM WOMAN
I AM
I AM A
I AM BLACK
I AM WOMAN
I AM
I AM
I AM
I AM JUST AS I AM
OR I AM
BECOMING
WHAT I AM....
AM I?

My Gift

My sensuous lips are mine
Passionate luscious
So voluptuous
So full
I am so fine
I am one of a kind
An ace and not too many outside
Of my race are blessed with
the lips on my face
I got a perfect set of
Soup coolers
Love rulers
Skin soothers
Heart 'fooler'
Conversation pieces
Beautiful and unique
And attached to match my psyche
So neat
My brown meat
Fully packed and
So Sweet
A mean and lean
Sexy dream machine
A Queen
Full of
Words
Curves
Muscles
Nerves
Stamina, assurance
And endurance
Are you blessed with my gift?
Some big pretty juicy lips
And hips that dip like mine?

Escape to Nowhere

penetrating music
body lying
calmly waiting
for my soul
to return
from my escape from
nowhere
music stops
I'm lying on floor
escapement still
going on while
computer fussing
printer too
projects unfinished
housework too
scattered books
thoughts too
paper everywhere
albums too
remote controls lost
mind too
and brains blowing
like curtains hanging
like painting too
nightlights bright
and flickering
stereo lights too
and the voices
next door bickering
while the goldfish
splashing and
turtles too
the music stops
escape does too

Unknown

When you fall in love
the feeling is there
the feeling is obvious
then there is a part of you
that wants to hold back
afraid of the unknown
what lies ahead
rules, vows and commitments
dos and don'ts
lifestyle changes
money arrangements
limited engagements
love can cause you happiness
as well as bring you pain
when you fall in love
you fall into an unknown zone

You Nurture Me

I love the way you
love me and how
you nurture me
You let me grow
physically
mentally
spiritually
keep watering me so
I can be free
and I can reach
out and extend
my roots deep
in the ground
continue to shower
me with positive
sayings, praying
and ravings
and satisfy my
cravings
so I can be confident
like the tall trees
fertilize me with love
and talk to me every day
warm me with sunshine
from your eyes, heart…
and soul

Send My Love

Slowly he walked out the door
He's gone, I'll never see him anymore
He was the counterpart of my heart
I have always loved him from the start
Now he is gone forever
Our experience, I will treasure
I will try my best to get him back
I know he won't give me any slack
I did him wrong and I regret it
For the rest of my life this I won't forget
He found out about his friend and me
He asked was I cheating; I had to lie. You see…
He walked in and caught us in action
His facial expression showed a terrible reaction
Deceived by his lover and friend
Wherever he's at my love I send
For the rest of my life I will grieve
Because the thought of my true love I deceived

No More Monsters

Many people can't understand why he loves the little children but will not breed his own

He tells them that he is happy giving to other people's kids and the people don't believe it's true just because he does not want to produce any monsters

I know where he comes from. He is a monster, because his dad is a monster. His mom and dad conceived and bred a monster. He battles daily with his monster to show the world that he refuses to be a mean monster

The world is already full of little monsters who come from bigger monsters. He reaches out to these little monsters to show them the way to kill their evil monsters so they can find happiness and inner peace

People need to understand that monsters breed monsters and suppressing a monster doesn't destroy the monster

And, yes, he is very happy, wanting to save little monsters and not wanting to bring any more monsters into this monstrous world

Spring

Snowstorms, sleet and ice, all over
A new season being born, I saw a clover
It's time for animals to birth their offspring
What a wonderful joy this season can bring
No more do we wear wool caps on our heads
But we still snuggle and bundle in bed
The beautiful sunlight has melted the snow
Once again the dreadful winter must now go
Flowers are blooming and grass turning green
Looking at it all is a beautiful scene
I remember this season when the birds start to sing
Summer, fall, winter, it's time for spring!

Second Time Around

You know I love you and our love was true
Is that the reason you do the things you do?
In love I thought we were, we've been together
for so long

So much fun we had, didn't know I'd get done wrong
You no longer want to be my lover or friend
How often you told me you loved me, was it for pretend?

Frequently I made mistakes and have my faults
I am changing and growing, I love you, keep the thought
Never have I slept without dreaming of you
Throughout the night

You are not my first love only the truest
After our relationship end you made me feel the bluest
I'll always love you even if you don't love me
It hurts me to see you go on, you are now free

Not only did you break my heart, you made it crumble
My hollow chest needs a heart, you can stop the grumble
Take me back because I'm feeling mighty down
Our love can be much truer the second time around

Our Calendar

In the bitter cold of January
You were a figment of the imaginary
Thinking back to snowy February
I did not have a sweetheart to marry
I remember my thoughts in windy March
Dreaming of someone like you to touch my heart
In the warm showers and flowers of April
It felt like meeting someone I was truly incapable
It was a very sunny and peaceful day in May
I knew if I prayed there would be a special day
It was very hot as I became anxious in June
I knew I just had to meet someone soon
We met on the fourth of July
The fireworks sparked the perfect guy
We had lots of fun in August
We never fought nor cussed nor fussed
During the month of September
Our love was still there to remember
I'll never forget the wonderful October
My luck is good without a four-leaf clover;
On Thanksgiving day in colorful November
Your prayer thanking God for me and the dinner
And looking back on our first Christmas
Under the mistletoe we had our first kiss...

The Scary Hair Story

Once upon a time before I found myself…I used to cry about it...Now, I laugh about it….Enjoy!

I got hair
Like a sponge
It is no fun
I can't run...

And play in the rain
No rain games
If I want to keep
My beauty and fame
And young men
Hollering my name

'Cause this puffy tangled stuff
Makes me fuss as it sucks up all the rain
It lacks 'cause it doesn't fall
Straight and flat and down my back

As a matter of fact -'cause of my luck
I got to pay big bucks
For hairdos that do this and that
To match the fly clothes on the designer racks

To look cute like the forbidden fruit
Those dream girls. My arch enemy
Listen…here is the skinny…

Those itsy-bitsy pearly model girls
Who appear in dreamy scenes in glamour magazines
With all those naturally curly and straight dos
That make my man go woo woo woo
Drives me freaking coo coo coo
'Cause I want one of those

Dos dos dos–too too too
Don't You You Yoooouuu?
I'm so blue blue blue
And I know that I have to learn
Who I am and become proud of
My natural hair and be
True true true but for now
The tangles gots to go go go …
You know...you know...you know...

The rain is driving me insane
So a girl of mine I looked up
Gave me the hook-up.
A new super perm-bone straight
The label reads–*no water can penetrate*
Apply now do not hesitate
Why wait?

So I am gonna test this mess
I run into the rain
Got tangles again
I can't win
Nevertheless–
Don't feel blessed

The weatherman says it will be a sunny day
No clouds, no showers, no sprinkles
I smiled and my face released the wrinkles
Now I got the power…In and out the shower
Dressed and out the door within one hour

Drove past a fly girl with the wind blowing
Through her super-long faked glued-on flowing hair
I had to stare as I thought …
Girl, don't you know I will have that look real soon?
That's Right! Right around noon
And my butter will fly 'cause I will be out of my cocoon

Driving fast, need gas but not making any stops
'Cause I got to get back to the beauty shop
To get it hooked up right. Darn. I just ran… the red light
My beautician wraps it super tight
Gonna have a hard time with sleep tonight
But I got to keep it like that 'cause that
'Do rag' will keep it silky straight without
The greasy looking mat and no need for a hat

My man can't make love to me
Or touch me tonight 'cause
If he mess with my hair
I will give him the evil glare
I get real mean 'cause
I have to get ready for tomorrow's scene
After I finish the touch with a mist of oil sheen

Now I am afraid of the rain like it bites
And I know that 'ain't' right
And I know that it's a shame
That I am a dame who thinks
My natural mane is lame

But I snap, Whatever!
'Cause I 'ain't' about giving up
My perm despite the fact
That I'm going insane
Because I left my umbrella
And the weatherman lied 'cause
Darn it, it's about to rain ...

Green-Eyed Monster

She stumps around envying me
I can't recall what I did to thee
I try hard to be the best of friends
She still gets mad again and again
I tell her my secrets to keep them hid
She blabs them out like a big-mouth kid
She's always trying to make up a contest
Only hates me more when I come out the best
I know that she has big green eyes
When I get something new she starts to cry
I still don't know what I did to her
Maybe she's a jealous green-eyed monster

It

There It was
tall and strikingly
beautiful
handsome too
fruitful
for I knew
before It knew
before we knew
that our love was true
but unaccepted
but we connected in time
now It is mine
not physically
not mentally
yes..spiritually
It took me where
no one else
dared to go
our moments
will be forever
embedded in my mind
and soul, and the details
of the passion goes
untold as the story
continues to unfold

The Good Life

every woman needs
to be greeted
and seated
and treated at
the spa
facials
spiritual cleansing
manicures
and pedicures for
the pretty feet and toes
and rings for her fingers
and toes
massages
fragrant body washes
sauna
hot steam and
milk baths
with rose petals
diamonds
always nicely treated
romantic
dinner
all are winners
that's the good life
yeah, that's right
that's the good life

Doomed to Die

Terrible pains awake me at night
Silently I lay, but in fright
May I not live until tomorrow?
Orally I pray, save me from sorrow
Physicians are baffled by my sickness
Maybe a curse for I have done wickedness?
The sun slowly rises in my dreary eyes
I lived through another night, I am surprised
My eyes water and I start to cry
I lived till morning but I still feel that
I am doomed to die

Stop Lying

why do people
especially our youth
say they want a family?
why in that lie they
continue to believe?
why are young boys
and girls so silly?
why do you really
think you are ready
and you are not
when you are hitting the spot?
now her little navel
is no longer a dot
and off to the clubs
or a new love he trots
and so will she when
the precious baby drops
neither one no longer
thinking of the little tot
so stop lying because
a little one is at hand
live up to your word
and be a woman and
man and always remember
that you are only hurting the
child so before you and your
partner begin to sin or mend
ask yourselves is a child
worthwhile?

Adolescence

I remember going through
A period that I once called blue
My adolescent stage…
Oh, what a challenging age
I needed to run wild and free
I absolutely hated being me
My parents kept me like a prisoner
Boys were not on the list for visitors
I was in a miserable position
My acne was not in a favorable condition
I could not wait until future birthdays
So the adolescent period would soon pass away
My moody attitude changed all day
Parents and elders I disobeyed
When I hung out with many of my friends
Jealously was behind my innocent grin
Oh, now I am very old, feeble and gray
Wishing I could relive my adolescent days
As I sit in my chair rocking away…

Punishment

you are on punishment
until school is out and
you will not get off
and that's no doubt
you can't watch TV
or talk on the phone
I know you are mad
at Mommy and Daddy
and think we are wrong
but to your teacher you told a lie
now you cannot go and play outside
I know you wish your parents
were on your side
Instead we feel like
we want to tap your hide
plus look at this big mess
I know you know I am upset
'cause it is sunny and June
and now we have to clean this room
so be a good son and daughter per your father
and your punishment will be over soon
and you will be served ice cream
instead of broccoli at noon

Crazy Thoughts

Suicide inside
Oh, what a ride
Driving your brain insane
the negative thoughts
about your faults
run in front of a train
step into the fast lane
get murdered by thugs
overdose on some drugs
then you just need to go
you need to get away from here
or there that's all
then your crazy thoughts
would begin to stall
and down will come
all the barriers and walls..

Go for It

How do some
have the knowledge,
the instinct–the gift
to follow their dreams?
skip college
go for the gold
invest their time
and money
others don't
some won't
you don't
don't know how?
you continue to struggle to
believe in yourself
no support system
you can't think
with the end
in mind
I, too, was once that
kind who
talked jive and spit
and sat, and sat
all day and was
wasting my life
away until I prayed
one day
my dream came true
that is why
I am talking
to you
So my words
of wisdom
are that you
should go
for it too

Chocolate Covered Nut

Sometimes I feel like a nut
More often than not
They made me a nut
I wasn't born this way
I blame them
Will they always be born that way?
They hate me
They hate dark
They love nuts
They love chocolate
Especially chocolate-covered nuts
They created dark chocolate
Because it's good, like us
They couldn't take how they loved us
So they created white chocolate
To resemble them
But they changed nothing
They still eat and love the dark chocolate,
Especially the chocolate-covered nuts
They eat and digest us
They will eat and digest us until
There aren't anymore
No more nuts to cover
No more dark chocolate

Why Life?

Some say…
Life is pure hell!
Why continue to dwell
In a mixed-up world?
Others say, be happy
You could be worse off!
Perplexing are my
thoughts!
Is this all that life's
about?
People screaming!
People who shout!
People complaining!
People who doubt!
Some say there's a
heaven
There is a heaven above
The place for the doves
I do believe
In the superior judge
I was told not…
To question his works!
His reasons for seasons,
The starving Ethiopians,
The deadly poison
Of a scorpion!
Discrimination
Differentiation
Rape
Crimes of hate
Slavery
The Holocaust
Evil powers destroyed the
Twin Towers
The Wars
Divorce
It's very hard
Not to question
The function of
The world
I often wonder do we
have
To play this game of life;
To reach
Eternal peace,
Eternal life,
Eternal rest,
To be eternally blessed…

I Freed the Truth

I stood before the world
They were my audience
They were there to hear the truth
The whole truth
And they waited with bated breath
To hear what all had been concealed
To hear what I had denied
Though angel on the 'outwardside'
I had demons flowing through my veins
My heart was a slave; I had to set it free
No longer able to play the game
Too many lies to remember my own name
I no longer could conceal
I no longer could portray
Who I am not, who I wish I could be
I told them the truth
I told them who I am
Who I did not want to be
I no more told the lies
The demons started to die
My heart started to cry
For it was now free of the many years
Of carrying the burden
Living a life behind iron curtains
My world audience clapped; I collapsed
Once they revived me, they told me I was free

It's Not Over

I've finally realized my thoughts were not wrong
Our love was immense but now it's all gone
I just tried too hard to hold on to our relationship
Wanting to keep you close when you wanted to go on a trip
Our love was true but there was something we lacked
I should have realized it by the way you were holding back
You said your feelings were not because of another girl
But the thought of you not loving me twirls my world
My pushiness and persistence used to get you upset
But I will be the best you had, that you can bet
Sometimes I wish I would have never met you
All I feel since we have parted is a sad, sad blue
I take that back, I was blessed to have shared what we had
Since it is over I must try not be to so, so sad
I do not believe there's plenty more fish in the sea
I must become the lighthouse to find you and me
Who knows after all this tension cools down
You will travel the world and come back to this town
I have always believed in God and not lucky clovers
Therefore, my faith is telling me that we are not over

Escribo/Escribi

I write because I love the art of writing...
Or do I write because it's the only way
I know how to express what's on my mind?

If I write in Spanish will my words mean
the same or feel as heavenly divine?

If I could sing, I wonder would I still love to write
Or would I get up on stage and just blow the audience away
like a big fat blues singer or would I write my songs?

Because I love to write and not sing. Because I don't love
to sing but I love to write or because I can't sing.

I write thinking I'm getting a message across while I'm
living or I write thinking I'll be read when I'm dead.

Who knows why I write or whether my writing is good or
bad. I write because it feels good or it feels bad when I
don't.

Escribi.

Escribo is the Spanish conjugate verb meaning "I write."
Escribi is the Spanish conjugate verb meaning "I wrote."

Lost In Oz

I wanna go home…like Dorothy…I wanna go home…like Dorothy…I wanna go home…like Dorothy.

Unlike Dorothy, I clicked my heels, I clicked my heels more than three times. She escaped! Why can't I?

Unlike Dorothy, I clicked my heels, I'm still here. This house can never be no home.

Unlike Dorothy, when the storm is over, I'm not in Kansas. I'm still running around lost in Oz.

Unlike Dorothy, when I wake up, I'm having the same bad dream. The witch and her brew. The wizard is laughing too.

Unlike Dorothy, she didn't have no man to leave her here in this house alone. The storms released her happy home.

Unlike Dorothy, my lover, my husband, my life is all gone. Toto came back to that girl wagging his tail.

Unlike Dorothy, when I clicked some more, I'm still lost and alone. When I clicked a little harder, I broke my heel.

Unlike Dorothy, maybe it's my slippers, you know they don't shine. Maybe it's the rainbow; you know it's missing.

Somewhere over the…
Unlike Dorothy, I don't see the rainbow, I don't sing and I don't know the lyrics to the song!

Euphoria-Rastafarian Love

There was something mystical in the air
Still can't understand why I was there
Jamaica is where the traveled spirit come from
Sounds of reggae bouncing off the drum
Music from the band danced in their heads
The hair of the people was long and locked in dreads
The grass was continuously being rolled and lit
People passing it after taking deep and soothing hits
The clothes of the people had a color scheme
All of them wore something with red, black or green
The extra dark beer was constantly sold
The bartender smiled as the night unfolded
The leader of the band ran up on stage
He grabbed the microphone with such rage
His eyes were low from many different things
Different things that will make him feel like a king
He looked into my eyes as he sang the love songs
Any type of control I had was all gone
All of the girls were screaming over him
I wonder whether he try to love all of them
He reached out and pulled me by the hand
He asked very sweetly if I would be his new woman
I asked the Rasta, What about all the girls before?
He sang the reply in my ear-*You are the one I adore…*

I Can't Stand the Rain

I can't stand the rain, so much rain
all that rain made the ocean
and icebergs so gigantic
that sink big ships like the *Titanic*
frozen waves that form from cold and water
and rain and sit in the middle of nowhere
like me that sit in my
window and stare and glare
and smell the rain in the air
as I pray to God to make
the rain and pain go away
as the rain beats at my
windowpane and
simultaneously
at my heart's pain...
sometimes I can't stand
the rain when it storms
on the outside and that same
storm you see and hear
you can feel in the inside
how can two people live
together and make love
out of nothing at all
like pretty blue eyes now
weeping eyes that become
cloudy and drop rainy tears that
turn white satin pillows to rivers—
like the captains who trust their gods,
winds and sturdy boats and set sail
into the deep blue sea like boats
that sink into the deep blue sea
that formed from the rain
that I can't stand against my windowpane...

Our Portrait

As I stare at the portrait
on the wall
I remember like
yesterday, the day,
month, week, hour
and the very millisecond
of the second that we
posed for the sketch.
The morning was
exceptionally sunny and
bright. It was just right.
As I sat posing, oh, how I
prayed that life would
never rain on our
beautiful parade as my
shimmering eyes like the
moonbeams stared at the
young handsome artist as
he smiled while capturing
our youth and our hearts.
A piece of time that we
can only experience again
when we stare at our
portrait and reminisce of
days we miss. In my
prayers, I plead that our
love would stay as high
as our portrait on the wall
For our beauty and youth
would remain perfect like
our faces crystallized in
forever and never will
never ever come…
I asked God, where will
our love be a few years
from tomorrow?
Dear God, may our
portrait, like our love…
never end up
in the attic, or cellar or a
yard or garage sale,
shipping dock, an auction
block, garbage dump
or a resale shop or the
collector who removes
the portrait and finds the
real value in the
antiquated gold frame
May our portrait
everlasting dally
on the wall long after our
physical bodies are
gone…So our spiritual
beings
can continue to stare at
the portrait on the wall
from another world,
another land another time,
another moment in
another day

Precious Gems

This *"Truth"* is dedicated to
All the precious little children of the world...
Be strong! You are the future!

Children, Children, Children
Gather closely around me
More precious than rare stones
Priceless gifts you are to thee

A blessing to have you near
Listen to all I have to say
I will only speak of truth
Already numbered are our days

Life is lovely but temporal
Time must be used wisely
Cautiously take each step
Evil ones will despise thee

Others will want you to fail
They will often try to mislead
Get you to do worldly things
In order that you not succeed

Without you there's no hope
Be strong. You are our world
Be happy for what you are
Doesn't matter boy or girl

Children, children, children
Hidden treasures to uncover
Feel free to dream of dreams
A world is waiting to be discovered....

The World from My Room

I am all alone…in my dark room
sitting in the blackness
looking into the darkness of my private room
that I have ultimately outgrown
for I have found the key to myself
so every door in the world is now open to me
toward the light I will soon go...
until then-which will be
the beginning but now feels
like the end of my peering
out my window at a world so bloomed
that I once thought doomed
now with fresh eyes
my negatives are now positives
I watch the children laugh and play
and the couple so happy and gay
and my neighbor and her boyfriend
as he brings her roses she releases a grin
I smile back at the stars and Mars and the moon
as I walk toward my, no longer closed, door
where in comes the sunny light and even though
it is night the light is a pretty shiny bright but not at all
blinding…but, welcoming to my sight
I am walking toward the light
yes, toward the light that is warming and bright

A Note from the Author...

I would like to thank you for taking the time out to read my collection. Please send your comments and feedback regarding this book or share your story and poetry about how your life was changed by finding the light. I would be honored to attend poetry jams, slams, social events and book club meetings for further enlightenment and discussion. Thank you for your support!
Please E-mail Cheryl@CherylKatherineWash.com
or visit www.CherylKatherineWash.com

Ordering Information

My Private Room
I opened the door and there was light...

Cheryl Katherine Wash

ISBN: 0-9722795-0-4

To order copies of this book, please send $10.00 plus $3.00 (U.S. dollars) for shipping and handling. Please make money orders or checks payable to EbonyEnergy Publishing. Let us know if you want an autographed copy. You can also order copies on-line or by visiting

www.ebonyenergypublishing.com
www.amazon.com
Borders Books
Distribution: Baker & Taylor
Local bookstores can order by ISBN: 0-9722795-0-4

EbonyEnergy Publishing, Inc. (NFP)
A division of the GEM Literary Foundation
P.O. Box 43476
Chicago, IL 60643-0476
Email: books@ebonyenergypublishing.com

www.EbonyEnergyPublishing.com

Brings you the best dynamic collection of literature, poetry and illustrations filled with depth, humor, love and life...

My Private Room
I opened the door and there was light...
Cheryl Katherine Wash
ISBN: 0-9722795-0-4

One-to-One
A Sensual Romantic Serenade
Steve Wyndhawke
ISBN: 09722795-1-2

A Myriad of Emotions

Michelle Larks
ISBN: 0-9722795-2-0

Bold from the Soul
Spiritual Healing
Lillian E. Mitchum

ISBN: 0-9722793-3-9

Laugh Now, Cry Later...
A window to my soul
Fatimah Macklin

ISBN: 0-9722795-4-7

About The Author

Cheryl Katherine Wash

is a graduate of DePaul University and did graduate study at Columbia College, Chicago, IL

Cheryl was born, raised, and continues to *"love"* in Chicago with her family.

By: Cheryl Katherine Wash

My Private Room…I opened the door and there was light
The Revelation
The Greenest Eyes
Loving Your Beautiful Bronze Self
Black Angel of the House

Contributions:

The Light in the Dark by Eric I. Keyes, III
Lady Kennedy of Beverly by Kennedy Wash
The Things I Could Tell You by J.L. Woodson

EbonyEnergy Publishing, Inc. (NFP) A division of the GEM Literary Foundation is dedicated to spreading positive energy to a wide and diverse audience.